s
a
ke
he
nat
eci-
s for
with

LAUGHING ELEPHANT • 3645 Interlake Ave. North, Seattle, Washington, 98103

ISBN/EAN: 9781942334149

Copyright © 2019 Laughing Elephant
First printing • Printed in China • All Rights Reserved.

LAUGHINGELEPHANT.com

PARTY CAKES !!

Easy to Make Cut-Up Cakes
That put the **FUN** back in **FUNKY**

WRITTEN & REPURPOSED BY
BENJAMIN DARLING & DANIELLE MARSHALL

and now SOME BASIC CAKE TALK

First and foremost, Party Cakes is about having fun! Making a Cut-Up Cake is an activity that you, the cake maker, can do with your friends or family, and have a really great time doing so, all the while creating something unique and edible to share.

It's about candy, and frosting, and cake, and food coloring, and coconut flakes, lots and lots of coconut flakes!

Party Cakes is NOT about perfection, competition, exacting recipes, or using special tools (although all of these are fine in their place.)

If you follow the instructions in this book, and subscribe to the notion that a few well spent hours in the kitchen with yourself or a loved one should be a fun occasion, then the outcome will surely be a beautifully wacky, imperfect masterpiece; a fantastically funky cake, held together with frosting and coconut. It will look cool, taste great, and become the delicious conversation starter and bold party addition that it was always meant to be.

Ok?... Ok!

Let's throw an apron on,

Turn the music up,

And have some fun.

Use the recipes in this book for cake and frosting, use your own recipes, or use a mix and ready made frosting. Hey, its a cake, you can't really go wrong when the end game is deliciousness.

Cool cakes completely before cutting and decorating.

Using the diagrams in this book, measure and mark the cake with wooden toothpicks before actually cutting. Or just eyeball it!

Assemble all cake pieces on a serving tray before frosting, If you don't have a large enough tray, cover some heavy cardboard with foil.

To keep your serving tray free of frosting and coconut, tuck strips of wax paper beneath the assembled cake pieces before frosting. When you've finished, carefully slide these strips away, along with the spilled frosting and coconut. Eat the coconut and lick up all the extra frosting. Lie down on the couch until the sugar rush is over...

After your cake has been cut up, and the pieces have been arranged on your tray (protected by wax paper) It is time to frost. Your frosting will serve as the delicious glue that holds your various cake pieces together. When in doubt frost it out!

To start, frost the pieces together to hold; then frost all of the cut edges, leaving the tops and uncut edges for last.

Feel free to substitute your favorite candy for what is suggested in this book. No one is going to object to peanut M&Ms over Jujubes right?

If you are going to travel with your cake, place it in a sturdy, shallow cardboard box, not too much larger than the tray holding it.

Keep it cool! A warm frosted cake can be a hot mess.

If you are traveling with your party cake, carry your decoration candies with you, and decorate your cake with the final touches after you arrive at your destination. Plus you got some candy for the trip!

Final Fun Suggestion:
Feed the extra cut off cake bits to some local
ducks or parking lot birds and watch their love for you grow.

Works with kids and dogs, too.

It's as Easy as 1, 2, 3...

 1. Bake

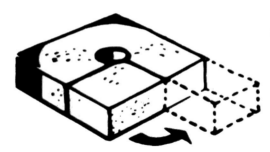 2. Cut

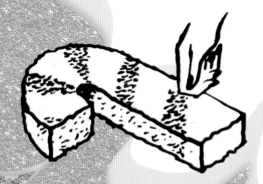 3. Decorate

CAKE RECIPE

The cake you Cut-Up can be made
from YOUR favorite recipe, from a cake mix
OR from this recipe here...

All the cakes use round 9 inch, square 8 inch
or 9 x 13 inch layer pans.
This recipe will make any of the three.

White Cake

Preheat oven to 375°. Have all ingredients at about 70°.
Sift before measuring:

2 ¼ cups cake flour

Resift with:

2 ½ teaspoons double-acting baking powder
½ teaspoon salt

Cream until fluffy:

1 ¼ cups sugar
½ cup butter

Add:

1 cup milk
1 teaspoon vanilla

Add the sifted ingredients to the butter mixture in 3 parts, alternating
with the liquid combination. Stir the batter until smooth after each
addition. Whip 4 egg whites (a pinch of salt makes them whip a little
better) until stiff but not dry. Fold them lightly into the batter.
When putting the batter into the pans, push the batter into the
edges and corners of the pans—the resulting cake will be more even
that way. Bake about 25 minutes, or until a knife or toothpick comes
out clean when inserted.

Seven-Minute Frosting

Yield: About 2 cups

This makes a beautiful fluffy frosting that is easy to use. It is easy to make if you have an electric mixer and a candy thermometer, because it is important to get the sugar syrup to the medium ball stage so that it cooks the egg whites to a firm consistency. Without a candy thermometer, the test is to draw a bit of syrup up out of the pan and see if it spins a long enough thread. If it won't, keep boiling the syrup until it does.
Mix thoroughly in a saucepan:

1 cup sugar
⅓ teaspoon cream of tartar
⅓ cup water

Boil slowing without stirring until syrup spins a 6-8" thread (242 degrees). Keep the pan covered for the first three minutes to prevent sugar crystals from forming on the sides of the pan. While the syrup is cooking, beat until stiff enough to hold a point:

2 egg whites (⅓ cup).

With the beater running at high speed, pour the hot syrup into the beaten egg whites in a thin stream.

Add 1 ½ teaspoons vanilla, and any coloring desired, and continue to beat for a few more minutes, until the frosting is the right consistency to spread.

Fluffy Chocolate Icing Yield: 2 cups

Beat together until fluffy:

2 cups sifted confectioners' sugar
¼ teaspoon salt
1 large egg
⅓ cup soft butter
2 oz. (2 squares) unsweetened chocolate, melted.

FROSTING

Quick White Icing

Yield: About 2 ½-3 cups

Beat until smooth:

3 cups sifted confectioners' sugar
½ cup soft butter
¼ teaspoon salt
1 ½ teaspoons vanilla
1 egg white
4 to 5 tablespoons milk or cream

If the icing is too thin add more confectioners' sugar

If too thick add a little cream or milk

Coconut!

A standard package of supermarket coconut has 2⅔ cups of coconut, one package of coconut will cover any of the cakes in this book. But always feel free to add more!

To toast coconut spread thinly on a baking pan and place in a 350° oven 8-10 minutes or until lightly browned. Stir or shake pan to toast evenly.

Food Coloring:
There are many types and strengths of food coloring out there. These recipes were designed to use a few drops from standard food colorings in red, yellow, green and blue. But feel free to use your imagination and any coloring you have on hand!

To tint coconut. Dilute a few drops of food coloring in a tablespoon of water in a bowl, add coconut and stir until tinted. Or put water and food coloring in a jar and add coconut, shake until coated.

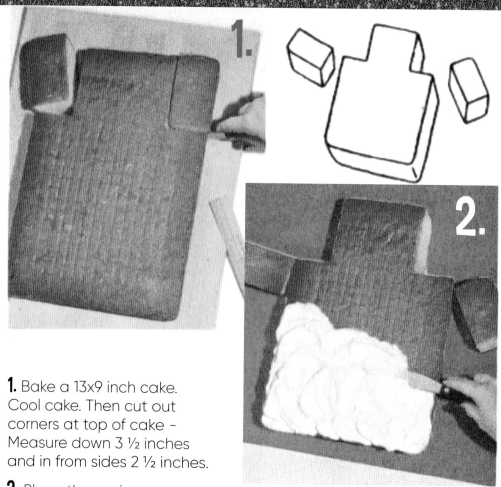

1. Bake a 13x9 inch cake. Cool cake. Then cut out corners at top of cake – Measure down 3 ½ inches and in from sides 2 ½ inches.

2. Place these pieces on tray as shown. When the snowman's arms are in place at sides, cover the entire cake with fluffy frosting. Swirl frosting on the head to make it look more round.

3. Now pat snowy-white coconut flakes over Mr. Snowman. Black gumdrops make good "chunks of coal" for his eyes, nose, and buttons – and a red gumdrop for his gay smile.

HERE'S A SNOWMAN THAT WILL JUST MELT IN YOUR MOUTH!

MR. SNOWMAN

3.

SWEETHEARTS CAKE

1. Bake a 9 inch round cake and an 8 inch square cake. Cool cake. Place square cake with one corner at bottom of serving tray. Cut round cake crosswise in half place cut sides of cake halves next to adjacent sides at top of square cake, to resemble heart.

2. Use some frosting to secure cake pieces to each other. Frost cakes with remaining frosting.

3. Tint coconut pink with food coloring; apply liberally over frosting. Decorate with fun red candies.

SHARE THE LOVE!

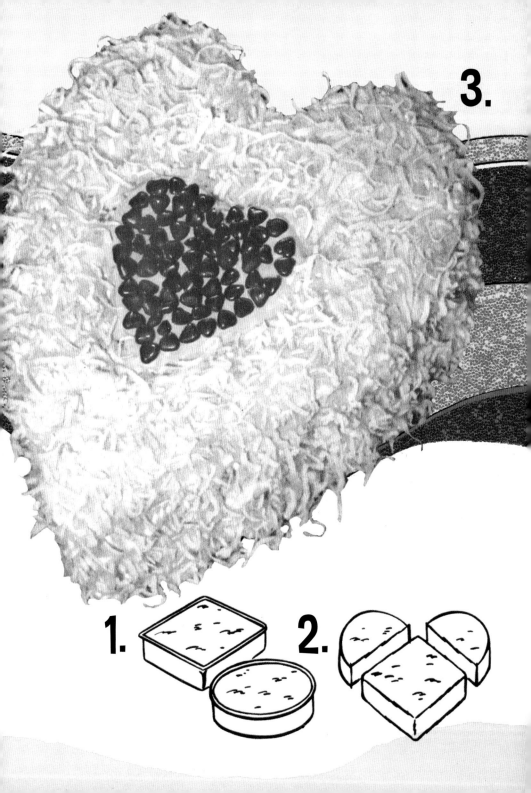

APRIL SHOWERS CAKE

3.

1.

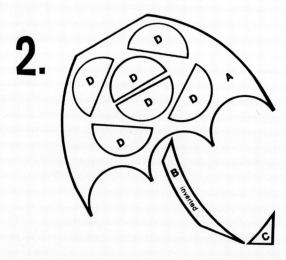

1. Bake a 9x3 inch cake. Cool cake. Measure and cut as shown above. Split each of the three **D** pieces through the center to make six equal pieces.

2. Arrange pieces **A**, **B** and **C** on a large tray and lightly frost. Position **D** pieces as as shown (they add volume to the umbrella.) Apply lots of frosting to entire cake.

2.

3. Color the umbrella sections with coconut tinted yellow, pink and green. Outline with licorice laces and add flowers made of mint patties and gumdrops.

SING IN THE RAIN WHILE EATING CAKE!

EASTER BASKET CAKE

1. Bake two nine inch round cakes. Cool cakes.

2. Frost between layers, on the top and sides. Stack cakes. Cut round cookies (Nilla wafers or any round wafer will do) in half. Stand the cookie halves around the edge of cake by pressing into the frosting. If necessary, support outside of cookies with toothpicks.
Frost the cookies.

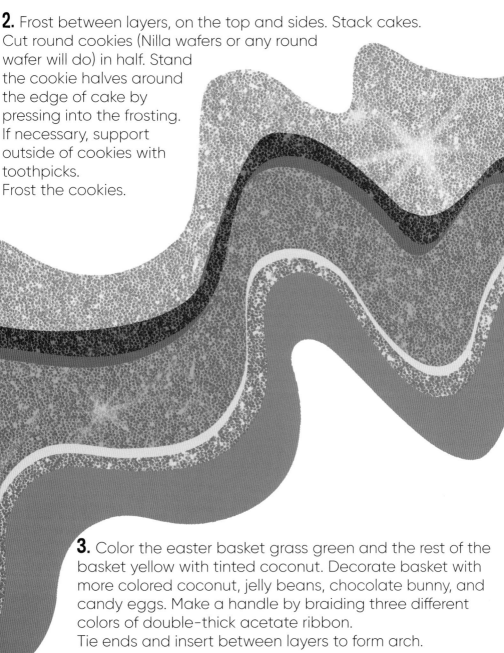

3. Color the easter basket grass green and the rest of the basket yellow with tinted coconut. Decorate basket with more colored coconut, jelly beans, chocolate bunny, and candy eggs. Make a handle by braiding three different colors of double-thick acetate ribbon.
Tie ends and insert between layers to form arch.

HOORAY! YOU MIGHT "WIN" EASTER WITH THIS FANTASTIC CAKE!

BOW TIE BUNNY

3.

1. Bake a 9 inch round cake and an 8 inch square cake. Cool cakes. Cut strips from opposite sides of an 8-inch square cake, 1 inch wide at top, 2 ½ inches at bottom. Cut a piece from each strip as illustrated to make ears floppy. Cut remainder of square cake as shown.

2. Arrange pieces on tray with 9-inch round layer as head. Frost heavily. Sprinkle tinted pink flaked coconut lavishly over bunny.

3. Decorate with red and white candy for eyes and nose, licorice for mouth, chiclets for teeth. Stripe Bunny's body and arms with a little more white icing.

MAYPOLE CAKE

1. Bake two 9 inch round cakes. Cool cakes. Stack cakes, measure and cut a 2 inch circle in the center of the cakes (a biscuit cutter is handy tool for this.) Cut the rest of the cake into 8 equal wedges.

2. Cover each cake piece with white frosting. Arrange cakes on a tray with a 1 inch space between each piece.

3. Sprinkle white coconut on the center piece. Tint the remaining coconut in pastel colors and drift the feathery flakes over the tops and outsides of the cake wedges. Twine ribbons from a center candy stick maypole, to small candy stick poles on each cake wedge.

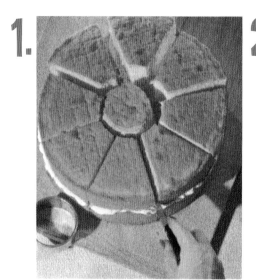

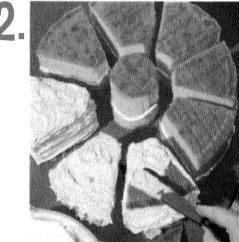

3.

BEAUTIFUL BALLOON

1. Bake two 9 inch round cakes. Cool cakes. From the diagram:
C makes the balloon. **B** makes the bottom of the basket.
A gets split through the center to make two identical pieces for the top of the basket (extra bits get eaten!)

2. Position both cakes on a large tray; swirl on frosting.
Stripe the balloon with plain and tinted shredded coconut.
Cover basket completely with yellow-tinted coconut.
Stow on board some doll passengers! Tie balloon to basket with licorice laces and decorate with more licorice and pastel candies.

BUTTERFLY CAKE

1. Bake a 13 x 9 inch cake. Cool cake. Cut off a 2 inch strip from short side of cake. Cut diagonally to form four triangles.

1.

B

A   A   C

B

2.

B

B

C   A

A

2. Arrange Cake pieces as illustrated and frost completely. Tint 1 ½ cups of coconut pale yellow and sprinkle over butterfly.

3. Decorate with candy, gum drops and jelly beans for butterfly wing markings, black licorice laces for antennae.

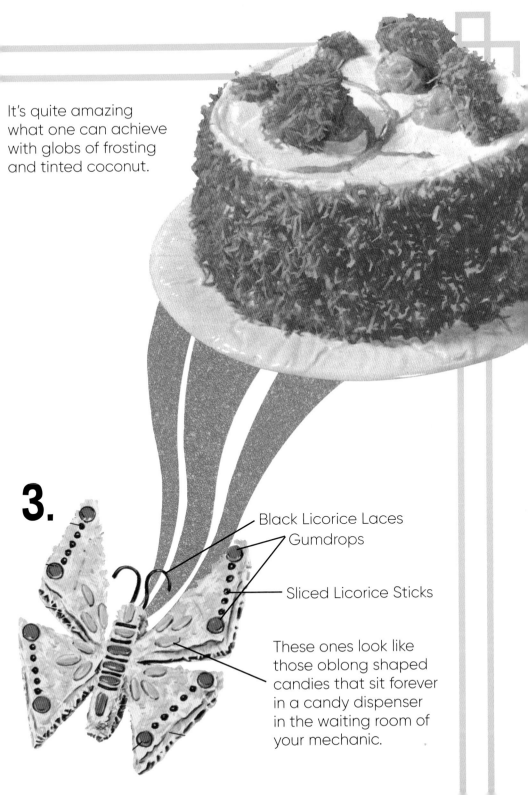

It's quite amazing what one can achieve with globs of frosting and tinted coconut.

3.

Black Licorice Laces

Gumdrops

Sliced Licorice Sticks

These ones look like those oblong shaped candies that sit forever in a candy dispenser in the waiting room of your mechanic.

ELLA ELEPHANT

1. Bake two 9 inch round cakes. Cool cakes. Cut a ring 1 ½ inches wide from the outer edge of one cake. Cut out a third of the ring for her trunk. Divide remaining piece of ring into four equal parts.

2. Place uncut layer on a tray for the body. Use the small circle for Ella's head. Add legs and a happy trunk.

3. Frost with pink frosting and sprinkle with coconut that has been tinted pink. Use a big chocolate cookie for her ear... gumdrops for the eye and toes, a cashew for her tusk, and a twist of licorice for the tail and eyebrows.
Throw a peanut in her trunk for a truly special touch!

WONDER ABOUT THE ORIGIN OF PINK ELEPHANTS, SHRUG, CONSUME CAKE GLEEFULLY!

1.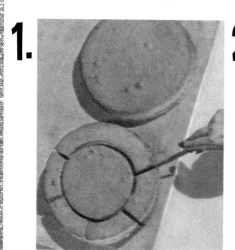

2.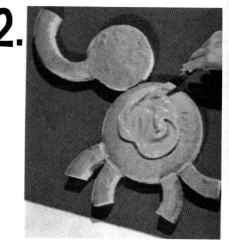

3.

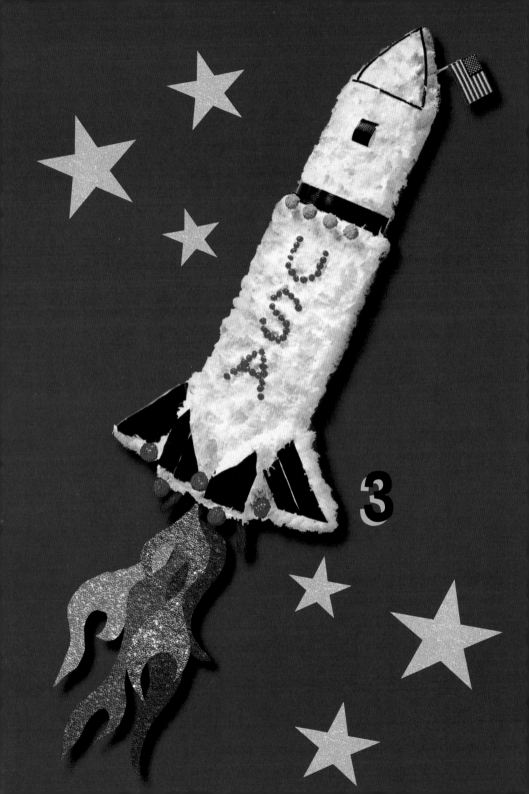

THE SPACE SHIP

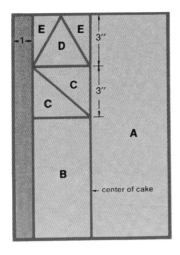

1. Bake a 13 X 9 inch cake. Cool cake. Cut cake in half lengthwise. Now, cut off and discard (by discard we mean eat) strip from long side. Finish cutting into sections shown.

2. Assemble Space Ship on a large tray. Spread small amount of frosting between cake pieces to hold. Spread rest of frosting over the entire cake, and sprinkle with coconut flakes.

3. Place pieces of black licorice on rocket as shown. Spell out U.S.A. with red cinnamon candies, and add "thrust" with red stick candy. FInish decorating with red and white gumdrops, dipped in water, then rolled in red sugar and blue candy sprinkles, respectively.

ROCKET INTO THE CAKE DIMENSION.

DAISY CAKE

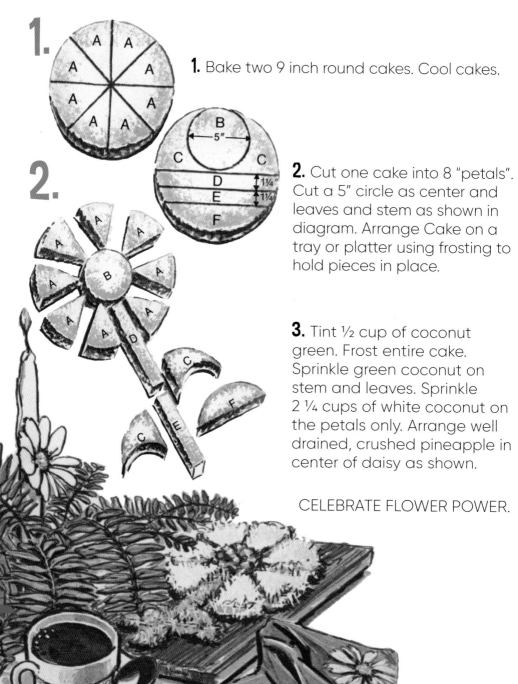

1. Bake two 9 inch round cakes. Cool cakes.

2. Cut one cake into 8 "petals". Cut a 5" circle as center and leaves and stem as shown in diagram. Arrange Cake on a tray or platter using frosting to hold pieces in place.

3. Tint ½ cup of coconut green. Frost entire cake. Sprinkle green coconut on stem and leaves. Sprinkle 2 ¼ cups of white coconut on the petals only. Arrange well drained, crushed pineapple in center of daisy as shown.

CELEBRATE FLOWER POWER.

3.

1. Bake an 8 inch square cake. Cool cake. Cut cake diagonally in half to make two triangles. One is the large sail. From the other, cut off a strip 2 ¼ inches wide to use for the hull.

2. Arrange cake pieces on tray, as shown, using the small triangle as the second sail. Spread white frosting on sails and cover hull with chocolate frosting. Put a line of chocolate frosting between the sails for the mast.

3. Sprinkle shredded coconut on the sails. White candies make neat portholes and gumdrops are easily cut into an anchor and a crescent for the sail.

SET SAIL FOR DELICIOUSNESS!

SAILIN' DOWN THE BAY CAKE

3.

SCHOOL HOUSE CAKE

1. Bake two 8 inch square cakes. (Put 2/3 of the cake batter into one pan and remaining third into the second pan.) Cool cakes. Cut the thicker cake in half, as shown above. Cut the thinner cake into four triangles.

2. Spread frosting, tinted yellow, on top of the rectangular cake pieces and stack them for the schoolhouse base. Put frosting on triangular cakes and arrange as the roof. When you've built your schoolhouse, frost with more frosting.

3. Thatch the roof with toasted coconut flakes. Make the windows and door with chocolate chips and chimney with a cookie. TInt more coconut green for grass and add a candy path and gumdrop bushes!

STUDY THE HAPPINESS A CAKE
THAT IS ALSO A SCULPTURE BRINGS!

HALLOWITCH CAKE

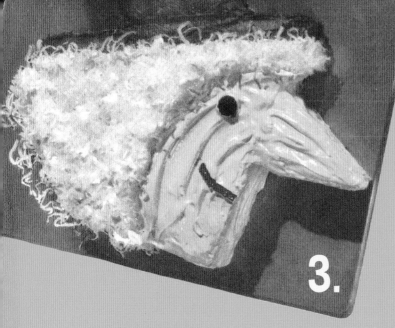

3.

1.

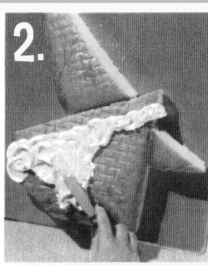

2.

1. Bake a 8 inch square cake. Cool cake. Measure 4 ½ inches down from corner and then cut diagonally across to opposite corner. The large piece is witches' face, the other is her hat. From shortest side of face piece, cut off a wedge 2 by 3 ½ inches to use for her nose.

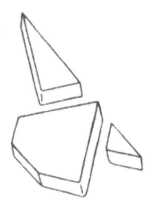

2. Place pieces on tray, as shown. TInt half of the frosting whichever color you'd like for face and nose. Spread white fluffy frosting – sprinkled all over with flaked coconut for hair. Her hat is chocolate frosting.

3. Candies make bewitching eye and mouth.

WHETHER SHE'S A GLAD WITCH OR A MAD WITCH IS UP TO YOU!

GOBBLE-GOBB-GOBBLER

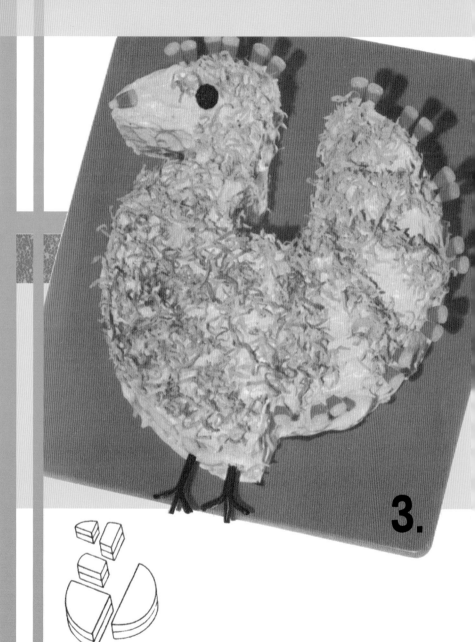

3.

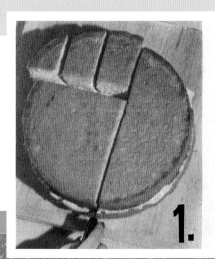 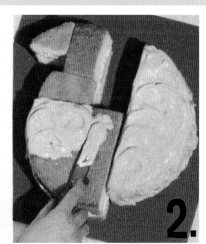

1. Bake two 9 inch round cakes. Cool cakes. Put fluffy chocolate frosting between the layers. Cut the cake in two pieces, making one 5 ½ inches (body,) one 3 ½ inches wide (tail.) Measure in 3 inches on the cut edge of large cake piece and cut across. Last, cut small piece into 3 strips of equal width (neck and head.)

2. Arrange pieces as shown in diagram. When Mr. Gobbler is placed on a tray, cover well with the frosting, swirling to look nice and plump.

3. Sprinkle on feathers of toasted flaked coconut. Decorate his tail with candy corn. Give him a candy eye and split licorice feet.

SANTA CAKE

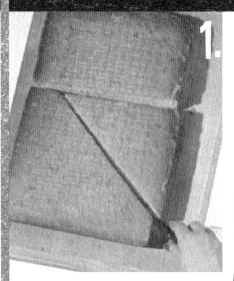

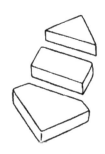

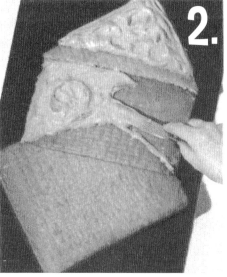

1. Bake a 13 X 9 inch cake. Cool cake. Cut a cross-wise piece from end of cake 4 ¾ inches wide, for Santa's face.

2. Cut across remaining cake, diagonally, to make a triangle 7 ¼ inches on two sides, for the hat and beard. Arrange cake on tray as shown.

3. Tint some of the frosting red and frost hat. Frost face with whichever color frosting you choose, making deep swirls for cheeks. Swirl the white frosting on the hatband and beard. Don't forget a frosting tassel for the hat. Make tassel, hatband, and Santa's beard look snowy soft with coconut flakes. Add laughing red candy mouth and sparkling blue candy eyes.

3.

SANTA SAYS, HO-HO HOLD ON TO THAT SLICE OF CAKE
I'M COMIN' TO TOWN!

DEER·IE the REINDEER

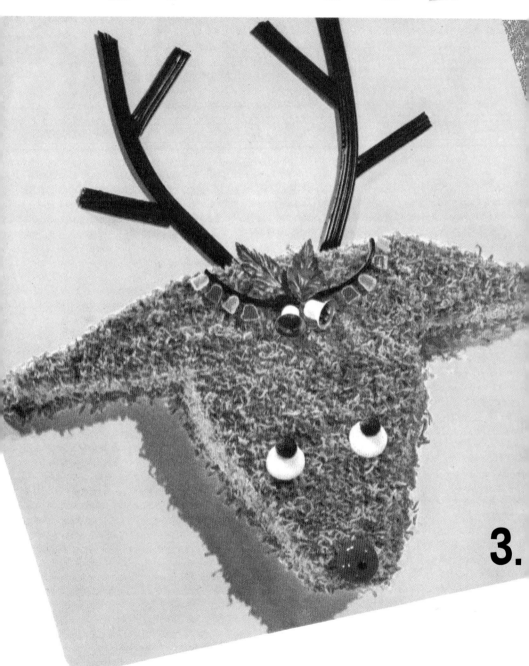

3.

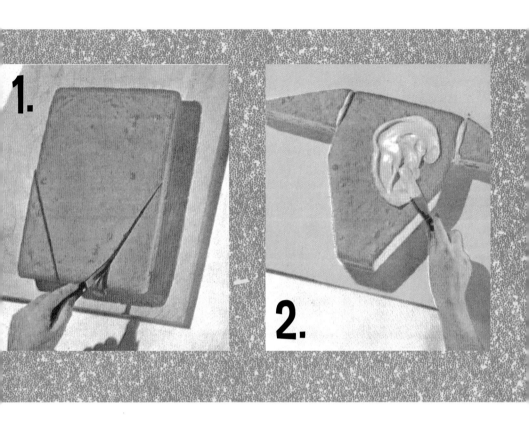

1. Bake a 13 X 9 inch cake. Cool cake

2. Measure in 3 inches along short side and 6 ½ inches up long sides from 2 corners. Cut through points to make ears. Place Ears on reindeer's head.

3. Frost with chocolate frosting. Use toasted coconut for face, and licorice sticks for antlers. Decorate using gumdrops, mints for the eyes and a small candy apple or large red gumball for his nose. The string of bells on Deerie's forehead is made with slices of small gumdrops.

ON DANCER ON PRANCER, ON CAKE, AND ON FROSTING!

CUT-UP

BAH
Bake
pan ir

To use
square
Then b
pans ab
9-inch s
ond 8-in
round la

Refrigera

CUTTIN
Mark mea
testers. Pla
you begin
large enoug
minum foil